Original title:
Northern Glow

Copyright © 2024 Swan Charm
All rights reserved.

Author: Kätriin Kaldaru
ISBN HARDBACK: 978-9916-79-717-4
ISBN PAPERBACK: 978-9916-79-718-1
ISBN EBOOK: 978-9916-79-719-8

## **Celestial Serenade on Ice**

The moonlight dances on frozen seas,
Stars are twinkling in gentle breeze.
Whispers of night in silver shades,
Echo through valleys, where silence pervades.

Beneath the blanket of icy white,
Dreams take flight on this serene night.
Cosmic tunes weave a magic charm,
Cradled by winter, safe and warm.

## Twilight's Embrace in the North

As shadows lengthen, the sun bows low,
A canvas painted in twilight's glow.
Whispers of twilight, soft and rare,
Wrap the world in tender care.

Frost-kissed trees in a tranquil stance,
Moonbeams glimmer, inviting a dance.
In the silence, secrets dwell,
Of the north's embrace, weaves a spell.

### The Gleam of Starlit Whispers

Under the veil of a starry night,
Dreams unfurl in celestial light.
Every twinkle, a story spun,
A spark of joy, where hearts are won.

The nightingale sings of love so true,
In the cosmic gardens where spirits renew.
Starlit whispers drift on high,
Carried softly on winds that sigh.

## Aurora's Kiss on Silent Peaks

In the stillness of dawn's first light,
Auroras dance, a breathtaking sight.
Nature's canvas in colors refined,
A symphony swirls, unconfined.

Mountains stand tall, adorned in grace,
Kissed by the magic of time and space.
With each glow, hearts ignite,
In the embrace of the morning's light.

## **Enigmatic Flickers at Dusk**

Shadows dance as daylight wanes,
Fleeting glimmers weave through veins.
Echoes whisper, colors blend,
The twilight's magic knows no end.

Voices linger in the air,
Mysteries float without a care.
Stars awaken, softly sigh,
In this moment, time slips by.

Glimmers tease the fading glow,
The heart beats fast, yet moves so slow.
Nature's secrets, gently spun,
In dusky realms where dreams are done.

## Lights of Serenity in Winter

Snowflakes drift on a silent night,
Candles flicker with soft delight.
The world is wrapped in blankets white,
A tranquil hush, all feels just right.

Stars twinkle above, so clear and bright,
The moon casts shadows, pure as light.
Whispers of peace drift in the air,
In winter's embrace, there's beauty rare.

The world slows down, takes a breath,
In this stillness, the heart finds depth.
Each moment cherished, softly spun,
In winter's glow, all worries shun.

## Serenity Under the Aurora

Beneath the dance of vibrant light,
Dreams are born, taking flight.
Nature's canvas paints the sky,
In the silence, spirits sigh.

Colors swirl, a cosmic embrace,
Each hue reflects a tranquil space.
The earth hums a gentle tune,
Under the watchful Northern Moon.

Whispers of wonder fill the night,
In this realm, all feels right.
Hearts unite in cosmic flow,
Under the aurora's wondrous glow.

## Ethereal Whispers of the Horizon

The sun dips low, a golden sigh,
Painting dreams across the sky.
Waves of whispers rise from the sea,
A symphony of calm, wild, and free.

Horizons stretch, vast and wide,
With every breath, the heart, our guide.
Fleeting moments, soft as lace,
In the distance, we find our place.

The world awakens in twilight's grace,
Life unfolds at a gentle pace.
Ethereal echoes linger on,
In the twilight where we belong.

## Whispers of Aurora

In the hush of dawn's soft light,
Colors blend, taking flight.
Gentle sighs across the skies,
Nature's secrets, low replies.

Crimson blooms and emerald haze,
Whispers of the morning rays.
Every wave of golden gleam,
Holds the promise of a dream.

Fluttering leaves in a cool breeze,
Dancing shadows beneath the trees.
Whirling whispers in the air,
Tell of magic everywhere.

Hearts ignite with passion's fire,
As the world begins to inspire.
In the light, we find our place,
Wrapped in nature's warm embrace.

## Beneath Celestial Canopies

Stars like jewels on velvet spread,
Carpet the night, where dreams are fed.
Moonlight drapes in silken threads,
Guiding us where silence treads.

Branches sway in a rhythmic dance,
Lost in a mystical trance.
Crickets serenade the night,
Nature's chorus, pure delight.

Shadows mingle with the light,
Underneath the starry sight.
Each flicker tells a tale old,
Secrets of the universe, bold.

Winds weave through the gentle air,
Whispering stories everywhere.
Beneath the vast celestial sea,
We find ourselves, wild and free.

## **Luminance in Winter's Embrace**

Crystal flakes in the frosty night,
Blanket the earth in purest white.
Whispers of chill in the air,
Softened shadows everywhere.

Fires crackle with warm delight,
Against the cold, a radiant sight.
Glowing embers rise and sway,
Chasing the shadows far away.

Echoes of laughter fill the space,
Winter's joy, a gentle grace.
In the hush of a silver moon,
Hope and warmth begin to bloom.

Snowflakes dance in swirling flight,
Cascading dreams in the soft twilight.
Each one unique, a fleeting kiss,
In winter's hold, we find our bliss.

## Dances of Celestial Light

In the twilight, stars ignite,
Chasing shadows, filling night.
Galaxies twirl, a cosmic ballet,
Painting dreams that drift away.

Comets streak with fiery trails,
Carrying whispers through the gales.
A waltz of planets, graceful sway,
In endless dark, they find their way.

Light cascades from far-off suns,
A timeless rhythm, never done.
Each twinkle sings of ancient lore,
Dances echo forevermore.

Wrapped in starlight's warm embrace,
Every soul finds its own space.
In the night, we learn to glide,
Dancing with the universe wide.

## **Celestial Echoes of the Frozen**

In the silence of the night,
Stars whisper tales untold,
Frost-kissed winds take flight,
Embracing dreams of old.

Moonlight dances on the snow,
Casting shadows soft and bright,
Echoes of a world below,
Wrapped in a blanket of light.

Crystals shimmer, glinting white,
Nature's breath, so pure, so still,
In the weave of dark and light,
Time pauses, bending will.

Chilling whispers through the trees,
Rustling leaves in frozen breath,
Nature's sighs stir with ease,
A melody of life and death.

Each heartbeat feels the chill,
As silence wraps the earth in dreams,
In this landscape, calm and shrill,
Celestial echoes weave their seams.

## Ephemeral Illume

Fleeting sparks in dawn's embrace,
Glimmering shades of gold and rose,
Light dances in an endless chase,
Whispers where the wild wind blows.

Moments caught in tender gaze,
Time drifts softly, never here,
Each flash a lingering phase,
A soft glow—a fleeting tear.

Petals fall, a gentle sigh,
Colors blend in softest hue,
Chasing shadows as they fly,
Life blooms bright, then bids adieu.

The sun dips low, a final kiss,
Painting skies in amber glow,
In its warmth, a sweet abyss,
Ephemeral, yet I'll not let go.

Memory hangs like morning mist,
Each heartbeat, bright as fleeting light,
In this moment, I persist,
Holding tight to soft twilight.

## Aurora's Heart on the Lake

Beneath the northern lights so bold,
Reflections dance on water's skin,
Colors mingling, stories told,
Whispers forming, deep within.

Night serenades the silent shore,
Ripples shimmer, secrets swell,
The lake breathes back forevermore,
In its depths, a timeless spell.

Stars awaken, twinkling bright,
Guiding dreams in gentle waves,
Aurora's heart ignites the night,
A tapestry of glimmering graves.

Fractured light meets stillness warm,
Every breath is filled with grace,
Nature hums a soothing charm,
In this dreamlike, sacred space.

Here, in stillness, souls unite,
The universe in harmony,
Aurora's heart, a radiant light,
Transforming night to ecstasy.

## The Spirit of Chilling Skies

Clouds gather like whispers near,
Carrying tales of winds unfurled,
Chilling skies, both wild and clear,
    Mirror secrets of this world.

Each gust breathes a ghost of frost,
Through the branches, shadows creep,
In this moment, dreams embossed,
    A lullaby that rocks to sleep.

Snowflakes twirl in frozen dance,
Painting earth with silent grace,
Nature sways in slow romance,
    Embracing winter's frigid face.

Stars peer down with ancient eyes,
Tales of light, both near and far,
The spirit stirs in chilling skies,
    Guiding hearts like distant stars.

Here in dusk, where echoes dwell,
In silence, secrets intertwine,
The spirit of the chilling spell,
    Awakens dreams that softly shine.

## **Painting Stars with Light**

In the hush of night, they gleam,
Brush strokes of silver, moonlit dream.
Each spark a whisper, tales untold,
A canvas of wishes, bright and bold.

Fingers trace the vast expanse,
Colors dance in starry trance.
Ink of the heavens, vivid and deep,
Awakening secrets that galaxies keep.

From cosmic wells, we draw our dreams,
Painting with starlight, or so it seems.
A palette of shadows, an artist's delight,
Every shimmer, a story, woven in light.

## **Frosty Echoes of Radiance**

Crystals twinkle on frosted ground,
Whispers of winter, a soft sound.
Moonbeams flicker in icy embrace,
Chill of the night drapes the space.

Echoes of laughter weave through the air,
As nature's magic dances with flair.
Every flake a note, pure and sweet,
Harmony found where silence meets.

In the hush, the world holds tight,
Glowing softly, the stars ignite.
Frosty dreams in silver hue,
A symphony sung, both old and new.

## A Glimpse of Cosmic Whimsy

In the realm where galaxies play,
A canvas of wonders, night and day.
Whispers of comets, trailing bright,
Spirits of the cosmos, taking flight.

Dancing nebulae twist and twirl,
Each star a secret, a gentle whirl.
Planets wear crowns of swirling light,
In this cosmic ballet, hearts take flight.

With every blink, a story unfolds,
Of ancient tales and dreams of old.
In this whirlwind of color and grace,
A glimpse of whimsy, our hearts embrace.

## Silhouettes Drenched in Aurora

Shadows stretch under a canvas bright,
Silhouettes move in the soft, pure light.
Auroras weave with delicate flair,
A tapestry painted in the cold night air.

Figures dance in ephemeral glow,
Beneath the arches, their movements flow.
Nature's brush paints with vibrant hue,
A dreamlike art, enchanting and true.

In the embrace of flickering skies,
Magic awakens, wonder replies.
Silhouettes glow, in this Aurora's thread,
An ethereal waltz, where dreams are bred.

## Shimmering Skies Above

In the dawn's golden gaze,
Colors dance, the world awakes,
Blushing hues across the haze,
Whispers of light, the night breaks.

Clouds parade in gentle forms,
Breezes carry tales so sweet,
Sunrise's magic, nature's norms,
Heartbeats quicken with each beat.

Birds take flight, a soaring crew,
Painting arcs against the blue,
With every splash, a vibrant hue,
Shimmering skies, forever new.

Harmony in each soft light,
Morning's joy, a pure delight,
In this canvas, futures bright,
Dreams are born for sheer take flight.

Every moment, a gift bestowed,
In this wonder, hearts decode,
Shimmering skies, life's true ode,
Underneath this vast abode.

**Luminous Veils of the Night**


Beneath the cloak of velvet skies,
Whispers glide on gentle dreams,
Stars are jewels, sparkled sighs,
Moonlight weaves its silver beams.

Shadows dance in quiet grace,
Softly cloaked in midnight's lace,
Echoes of a secret place,
Time stands still in this embrace.

Crickets sing their serenade,
A symphony of night's delight,
Every note a soft cascade,
Luminous veils, pure and bright.

Waves of starlight kiss the ground,
Painting silence like a song,
In this realm, our souls are found,
Into the night, we all belong.

Glistening paths of fading light,
Guide our hearts till dawn's own flight,
In the darkness, dreams take flight,
Veils of night, our guiding sight.

## Starlit Silhouettes

Underneath the endless dome,
Silhouettes of trees stand tall,
Casting shadows, nature's home,
In stillness, we hear their call.

Moonbeams touch the earth so light,
Guiding paths through dusky trails,
Softly glowing, hearts take flight,
In the night where magic prevails.

Whispers carried through the breeze,
Secrets shared with every sigh,
Time suspended, moments freeze,
Starlit dreams that linger nigh.

Figures dance, a fleeting view,
Lost in reverie's embrace,
Every heartbeat, something new,
Dancing shadows find their place.

Starlit silhouettes, whispers blend,
Moments captured, stories told,
In the night that will not end,
Magic weaves a tale of gold.

## **Chasing Dusk's Embrace**

As daylight fades to twilight gleam,
Colors merge in soft caress,
Chasing shadows, every dream,
Finding solace in the mess.

Hues of orange softly blend,
Crimson streaks across the sky,
Nature's canvas, colors send,
Whispers that begin to fly.

Gentle winds begin to sway,
Branches dance in fading light,
Each moment bids the day to stay,
But dusk calls in its sweet flight.

Stars ignite in velvet grace,
Artistry of night's embrace,
In the quiet, find your place,
Chasing dusk, a tender chase.

And as the sun dips low,
Fleeting glimpses as we go,
In twilight's arms, we softly sow,
Memories captured in the glow.

## **Twilight's Dance of Colors**

The sun dips low, a fiery glow,
Shadows stretch long, the night's soft show.
Crimson and gold paint the fading sky,
As whispers of dusk bid the day goodbye.

Stars appear, their twinkling light,
Guiding the dreams into the night.
Breezes carry the scent of pine,
In this serene hour, all feels divine.

Clouds dance slow in twilight's embrace,
Each hue a promise, a tender trace.
Nature sighs as daylight departs,
Kindling the magic within our hearts.

The horizon blurs in violet hues,
Painting the world in softened views.
As night unfolds her velvet cloak,
All is silent, as if time spoke.

With every breath, the night unfolds,
A tapestry rich, a tale retold.
In twilight's grasp, we find our peace,
As colors blend and worries cease.

## Ethereal Brushstrokes

A canvas wide, where dreams take flight,
Each stroke a whisper, soft and light.
Colors collide in harmonious play,
Crafting a world where spirits stay.

The palette sparkles under soft beams,
Inviting us into the realm of dreams.
Brushes dance with a painter's grace,
Creating illusions, a sacred space.

Pastel clouds float on skies so clear,
Invoking the hope that lingers near.
Ethereal hues blend, then expand,
Revealing the magic of a master's hand.

Every stroke tells a story anew,
From vibrant reds to tranquil blue.
With each creation, the heart sings loud,
In a gallery bright, under every cloud.

A masterpiece born from quiet thought,
In this tranquil space, peace is sought.
The beauty flows through every hue,
In ethereal brushstrokes, joy feels true.

## **Moonlit Reflections Beneath**

Silver beams cascade on rippling streams,
Painting the night with gentle dreams.
Reflections shimmer, a dance of light,
Guiding lost souls in the soft twilight.

The moon hangs low, a guardian bright,
Casting soft whispers of tranquil night.
Each wave a secret, every ripple a sigh,
In the cradle of night, where shadows lie.

A symphony played by the winds that blow,
Softly caressing the world below.
Branches sway in a rhythmic trance,
Under the glow, the heart finds its chance.

Silence reigns in this serene space,
As minds wander through time and place.
Moonlit reflections, a canvas so grand,
Where soulmates meet and forever stand.

Beneath the stars, in quiet repose,
The beauty of night tenderly grows.
In moonlit reflections, we find our way,
Guided by dreams, till the break of day.

# Echoes of the Arctic Sun

In the land of ice, where shadows play,
The Arctic sun paints the world in array.
Golden rays beam on pure white snow,
Creating a wonderland, vibrant and aglow.

Hushed whispers of frost curl in the air,
Nature's breath speaks of beauty rare.
Mountains rise tall, majestic and grand,
Guarding the secrets of this frozen land.

Icebergs drift softly, like dreams afloat,
Sculptures of nature, a delicate note.
Reflections dance on the crystal clear seas,
Echoing stories carried by the breeze.

Wildlife awakens beneath the bright sky,
With rhythms of life, as moments pass by.
In the stillness, echoes of joy ring,
Celebrating the warmth that the sun can bring.

As day fades gently into the night,
Colors dissolve in the fading light.
The Arctic sun, a beacon so bold,
Whispers of tales from the warmth of old.

## Hushed Voices Beneath the Stars

In silence we gather, shadows entwined,
Whispers of dreams in the cool night wind.
Under the blanket of shimmering night,
We share our secrets, lost out of sight.

A flicker of starlight, a soft, gentle gaze,
Moments of magic in delicate haze.
The universe listens, our hearts beat as one,
Beneath the vast sky, we feel so undone.

Echoes of laughter, stories unfold,
Woven together, both timid and bold.
The hush of the night holds our truths so dear,
In these shared whispers, we conquer our fear.

With every heartbeat, the cosmos aligns,
Guided by fate through celestial signs.
In hushed voices spoken, our souls are set free,
Under the stars, it's just you and me.

## Colors of Nightfall's Caress

As daylight surrenders, the canvas turns deep,
The colors of twilight begin to seep.
Velvet blues mingle with strokes of soft gold,
A beauty unfurls, a story unfolds.

Shadows awaken, the night breathes alive,
In hues of the darkness, our spirits will thrive.
Misty lilacs dance with the chill in the air,
In colors of nightfall, we find warmth laid bare.

The moon paints a path with its silvery glow,
Guiding our footsteps while memories flow.
Stars sprinkle the heavens, a glittering spree,
In nightfall's embrace, we are wild and free.

With every soft whisper, the world starts to dream,
A tapestry woven with threads of moonbeam.
In colors of nightfall, surrender your heart,
As night takes the stage, a brand new fresh start.

## Secrets Hidden in the Dawn

As dawn's first light breaks, a hush fills the air,
Soft whispers of promise, a world beyond compare.
Secrets of night linger, fading from view,
In the embrace of morning, all feels renewed.

Golden rays dance, brushing all they touch,
Awakening whispers, oh, how they clutch!
Each shadow retreats with a gentle embrace,
Revealing the secrets in time and in space.

Birds chirp their stories, a sweet symphony,
In the quiet of morning, they sing wild and free.
The dew on the grass sparkles, a tale to be told,
As secrets of night are turned into gold.

Awake is the world, a bright canvas unfurled,
Dreams carried gently, a new day is hurled.
With each passing moment, let go of the night,
For secrets in dawn bring a future so bright.

## Structural Patterns of Light

In beams of illumination, the patterns we find,
Light dances through space, leaving echoes behind.
A prism of colors, each angle a key,
Unlocking the beauty in all that we see.

Windows of wonder, they frame the divine,
Casting shadows and highlights, perfectly aligned.
From the flicker of candles to sun's warm embrace,
Structural patterns of light paint the space.

Through the golden hour, the landscape will change,
Sketching each moment, beautifully strange.
In every reflection, a story will bloom,
In structures of light, we can banish the gloom.

Through twilight's descent, patterns twinkling bright,
We trace constellations in the fabric of night.
The art of existence, from dawn to the end,
In structural patterns of light, we transcend.

## Phosphorescent Wonders

In the night, the glow ignites,
Beneath the stars, a dance takes flight.
Whispers of light in dark embrace,
Nature's art, a fleeting trace.

Rippling shades of emerald green,
Shimmering waves, a vibrant sheen.
Boundless beauty in silent grace,
Phosphorescent wonders, we chase.

Ocean depths hold secrets deep,
In tranquil tides, where shadows creep.
A flicker here, a spark there,
Life beneath, a treasure rare.

With every pulse, the world awakes,
In luminous hues, the silence breaks.
A cosmic show in twilight's hold,
Phosphorescent wonders unfold.

So let us wander, dare to seek,
Through hidden paths, where spirits speak.
In nature's glow, we find our way,
Phosphorescent wonders lead the day.

**Frosted Lanterns Above**

In winter's breath, the heavens glow,
Frosted lanterns, soft and slow.
Twinkling gems in velvet skies,
Silent wishes, whispered sighs.

Each star a beacon, bright and clear,
Guiding hearts, drawing them near.
With every shimmer, dreams take flight,
Frosted lanterns spark the night.

Snowflakes dance, a silvery rain,
Painting landscapes, pure and plain.
Beneath their light, our hopes arise,
Frosted lanterns in twilight skies.

In the stillness, magic we find,
Threads of wonder, softly entwined.
Embracing beauty, we remain,
Frosted lanterns, joy and pain.

So gather 'round and share the glow,
Underneath the lantern's show.
For in their light, our souls entwine,
Frosted lanterns, yours and mine.

## Celestial Veil over the Tundra

A mystic shroud, the sky unfolds,
A celestial veil, a tale retold.
Whispers of stars in the chilly air,
On frozen ground, magic lays bare.

Drifting snows in the moonlight's embrace,
A tapestry of beauty, time cannot erase.
In silence, the tundra softly sighs,
As shadows dance beneath the skies.

Glaciers shimmer, like diamonds bright,
In the heart of the night, we find delight.
The cosmos watches, serene and still,
A celestial veil, a gentle thrill.

Endless horizons in tranquil sight,
Wrapped in wonder, hearts take flight.
The northern lights with colors flow,
A celestial veil, a wondrous show.

In this realm where dreams collide,
Love and magic, side by side.
Forever cherished, ever true,
Celestial veil, a bond anew.

## **Light Play in the Frozen Kingdom**

In a realm where silence reigns,
Light plays tricks on icy chains.
Colors dance on crystal ground,
Echoes of joy in whispers found.

A flicker here, a shimmer there,
Nature's brush paints everywhere.
In the frozen kingdom, dreams arise,
Beneath the arch of endless skies.

Snowflakes drift like falling stars,
Caressing earth from distant wars.
In the stillness, wonder blooms,
Light play chases away the glooms.

Amidst the frost, our spirits soar,
Exploring realms unseen before.
With every step on glittering trails,
The frozen kingdom sings, prevails.

So let's embrace this magic bright,
For in our hearts, we hold the light.
In every shard of ice that gleams,
Light play weaves our frozen dreams.

## Frozen Echoes in Lush Wilderness

Whispers of frost in the morning light,
Silence wrapped in nature's embrace.
Echoes of life beneath the snow,
A realm where time holds space.

Icicles hang like crystal dreams,
Frozen tales of the woodland pulse.
The air is crisp with a glorious chill,
As shadows dance, the branches convulse.

A pathway bordered by silver pines,
The world asleep in a glistening quilt.
Unseen creatures beneath the frost,
In hidden realms where warmth is built.

Rushing streams are held hostage here,
Yet murmurs travel through layers deep.
Nature's heartbeat, a distant song,
A promise of life in the cold to keep.

The sun will rise, and thaw these lands,
Yet for now, let serenity reign.
In the frozen echoes, the wilderness sighs,
As dreams and memories gently remain.

## Visions of Ethereal Splendor

In the twilight's hold, colors collide,
A painter's brush across the sky.
Clouds like silk in a soft parade,
Where dreams unfold and spirits fly.

Glimmers of gold in the fading light,
Stars awaken, blinking bright.
Whispers of magic, secrets untold,
In shadows where fantasies ignite.

Mountains rise like guardians tall,
Reaching for stars in a velvet sea.
Moments freeze, as silence falls,
Crafted in time, eternally free.

Nature's canvas, a wondrous array,
A symphony sung by the evening breeze.
With every hue, the heart grows bold,
In this realm of ethereal tease.

As night unfurls its ebony cloak,
The world drifts into a reverie.
Visions linger in bewitching dreams,
Where splendor dances and souls agree.

## **Frostbitten Flames in the Sky**

When twilight descends, the air grows cold,
A clash of worlds in fiery hue.
Crimson glows beneath the frost,
A canvas alive, ever anew.

Frostbitten flames flicker and sway,
As night and day play their games.
The horizon burns with embered light,
While winter whispers forgotten names.

Stars emerge in diamond glints,
A cosmic dance in the frozen night.
Beneath the frost, there's warmth untold,
In the heart of darkness, hope ignites.

Shadows stretch like painted wings,
Kisses of light on a frosty cheek.
The flame of dawn will soon lay claim,
To a slumbering world so pristine, unique.

In this moment, twilight sings,
A harmony of dusk and flame.
Frostbitten dreams in the vast expanse,
Are memories of life, never the same.

## Celestial Miracles Above the Fjord

Above the fjord, the heavens gleam,
A tapestry woven of light so rare.
Miracles dance in an endless waltz,
As stars cascade through the chill of air.

Reflections shimmer on waters deep,
The moon's embrace ignites the night.
Whispers echo through mountain heights,
In this tranquil space, all feels right.

Auroras billow in colors bold,
Vivid strokes of a cosmic brush.
The earth stands still as wonder unfolds,
In the tranquil air where galaxies hush.

Clouds drift softly like dreams in flight,
Guardians of secrets held so tight.
Each gaze upwards ignites the soul,
With celestial miracles, pure delight.

Beneath the vastness of starlit skies,
The fjord reflects a world sublime.
In nature's beauty, together we sit,
In harmony, transcending time.

## Dusk's Embrace in the Chill

The sun dips low, a whispered sigh,
As shadows stretch to hug the sky.
Crisp air bites, a cool caress,
Nature holds its breath, no less.

Leaves rustle soft, a farewell tune,
The stars awake, a silver boon.
Night drapes all, a velvet cloak,
In this hush, the world awoke.

Moonlight spills on tranquil streams,
While crickets weave their sleepy dreams.
In dusk's embrace, hearts find their peace,
As day and night begin to cease.

Flickering shadows dance and sway,
Guided by twilight's gentle play.
Together they twine, unafraid,
Where every breath feels serenade.

Underneath the starry arch,
Wonders bloom, as night takes charge.
Embraced by dark, the world feels right,
In dusk's sweet grip, we find our light.

## An Odyssey of Twinkling Lights

Across the sky, a canvas bright,
Stars whisper dreams in the quiet night.
Each twinkle tells a tale untold,
Of journeys ventured, brave and bold.

Nebulae swirl in wondrous hues,
Painting the void with vibrant views.
A cosmic dance of fate and chance,
Inviting all to join the dance.

Comets streak like shooting flames,
Carrying stories, ancient names.
In their wake, a shimmering trail,
Guiding the lost, where hope prevails.

Galaxies spin in endless grace,
An odyssey through time and space.
With every blink, a wish takes flight,
Beneath the blanket of soft, pure night.

Together under celestial skies,
Hearts entwined, no need for lies.
In this expanse, we are set free,
An odyssey of life, you and me.

## Colors Resurrected in Darkness

In shadows deep where silence dwells,
A whisper paints the night with spells.
Emerald greens and ruby reds,
Come alive where light seldom treads.

Midnight blooms, a vibrant array,
Awakening dreams where night holds sway.
Each petal glistens with hidden grace,
Resurrected hues in a soft embrace.

The moon, a brush with gentle hand,
Colors the world, a silent band.
From darkest night, true beauty springs,
In the hush, the heartache sings.

Rippling shadows, each hue refined,
A kaleidoscope of love defined.
In darkness found, all fears will cease,
Colors resurrected, bring forth peace.

So let the night enfold you whole,
And splashes of dawn reclaim your soul.
In every shadow, there's life anew,
Colors resurrected in the view.

# Resonance of Starry Nights

Whispers of the darkened sky,
Stars twinkle like a lullaby,
Dreams drift in the silent air,
Echoes linger everywhere.

Moonlight dances on the lake,
Rippling soft, like dreams awake,
In the stillness, hearts entwine,
Finding solace in the divine.

Constellations tell their tales,
Guiding ships through whispered gales,
Hearts pulse with the cosmic flow,
In the night, our spirits glow.

The universe, vast and bright,
Cradles us in its embrace tight,
Every star a hopeful spark,
Illuminating realms so dark.

Through the quiet, love will soar,
In the resonance, we explore,
Infinite dreams, forever bright,
Lost in the starry night.

## **Frozen Horizons**

Endless stretches, white and blue,
Whispers of the cold wind's view,
Footprints mark the snow-clad ground,
In silence, beauty can be found.

Icicles hang like nature's art,
Framing scenes that warm the heart,
Frosted breath beneath the sun,
Chasing shadows, one by one.

Mountains rise with noble grace,
Guardians of this frozen place,
Skies reflect the shimmering glow,
In winter's clutch, our spirits grow.

Silent nights with stars aglow,
Nature's canvas set to show,
Blankets woven thick with dreams,
In the stillness, magic beams.

As dawn kisses the world awake,
Colors blend, reflections break,
Life bursts forth in every hue,
In frozen horizons, hope is true.

## Magic Beneath a Velvet Sky

Underneath the twilight's cloak,
Murmurs rise, softly spoken folk,
Glow of fireflies, stars ignite,
Painting wishes in the night.

Whispers dance on moonlit streams,
Carrying the weight of dreams,
While the night winds serenade,
Magic stirs beneath the shade.

Crickets play their lullaby,
Nature's tunes, they never die,
Every heartbeat finds its way,
In the dark, our spirits sway.

The sky, adorned with shimmering lights,
Holds our secrets, love ignites,
In the hush, we find our bliss,
Sealed forever with a kiss.

Beneath the velvet, worlds unite,
In the magic of the night,
Dreams take flight on silken wings,
In this moment, the heart sings.

## Glows of the Icy Expanse

Underneath the frosty glow,
Branches twist with winter's flow,
Crystals shine in moonlit grace,
Icy wonders fill the space.

The stillness wraps the night in white,
Every star a sparkling sight,
Winds whisper secrets old and new,
In the expanse, dreams come true.

Frozen lakes, so bright and wide,
Reflect the beauty of the tide,
Nature paints with strokes so fine,
In the cold, our hearts align.

As dawn breaks with a golden hue,
Bringing warmth to every view,
Eager eyes explore the scene,
In the icy backdrop, love gleams.

Through the chill, we share our light,
Together in this wondrous sight,
In the glows, our spirits dance,
In the icy expanse, there's romance.

## Radiant Whispers in the Snow

Softly falls the snow so white,
Whispers dance in winter's light.
Branches bow with crystal tears,
Echoes of forgotten years.

Footprints trace the path we take,
In the hush, our memories wake.
Frozen dreams in silver glow,
Nature's peace, a silent show.

Stars above twinkle so bright,
Guiding hearts through the cold night.
Underneath the moon's soft gaze,
Hope ignites in winter's haze.

Each flake tells a story deep,
In the stillness, secrets keep.
Radiant whispers, soft and clear,
In the snow, I hold you near.

## Dancing Flames of the Faraway

Flickering shadows, wild and free,
Dancing flames call out to me.
In the night, their stories spin,
Of worlds beyond, where dreams begin.

Embers soar like shooting stars,
Igniting hearts, erasing scars.
Through the smoke, our spirits rise,
Boundless joy within the skies.

Crisp air carries tales untold,
Of adventures, brave and bold.
A flicker hints at distant lands,
Where hope glows bright in gentle hands.

In every blaze, a wordless song,
Calling out, we all belong.
With every spark, a bond we tether,
We dance together, forever.

## Ascendance in an Icy Realm

In the frozen silence, we arise,
Amidst the chill, we touch the skies.
Crystals shimmer in the pale light,
Guiding souls through the endless night.

Mountains gleam like ancient lore,
Where time stands still, forevermore.
Each breath, a cloud of dreams in flight,
Carried forth on the wings of night.

Through the frost, we seek the dawn,
In icy grasp, our fears are gone.
Ascendance flows like river's song,
In this realm, we all belong.

Stars like diamonds, bright they gleam,
Casting wishes on a dream.
In the depths of winter's breath,
We find our strength, defying death.

## Night's Embrace of Light

In the velvet cloak of night,
Stars awaken, pure delight.
Moonlight bathes the world below,
In its glow, our shadows grow.

Whispers float upon the breeze,
Carrying the night's soft pleas.
Time suspends—a gentle sigh,
As dreams unfurl, like wings, to fly.

Each heartbeat echoes in the dark,
Painting silence with a spark.
Night's embrace wraps us in grace,
Finding warmth in this still place.

Dancing light on rivers deep,
Secrets held in stars we keep.
In the stillness, all feels right,
As we bathe in love's pure light.

# Veils of Luminescence

In twilight's hush, whispers gleam,
Veils cascade, weaving a dream.
Softly they dance in the night,
Embracing shadows, kissing light.

Stars above in endless grace,
Paint the sky, a vast embrace.
They shimmer, flicker, and play,
Guiding souls along their way.

Mysteries in the silent air,
Secrets linger everywhere.
Beneath the moon's gentle gaze,
Hearts entwined in glowing maze.

Hope unfurls like wings of dawn,
In light's embrace, fears are gone.
Each heartbeat sparkles, anew,
Awakening dreams born of dew.

In luminescence, love ignites,
A tapestry of perfect sights.
In every sigh, every glance,
Life's magic thrives in this dance.

## A Canvas of Northern Light

Streaks of green in darkened skies,
A canvas vast, where beauty lies.
Brushstrokes from the cosmic hand,
Dance above this frozen land.

Whispers of the Arctic breeze,
Play with shadows, sway the trees.
Colors blend in swirling art,
Nature's palette, every heart.

Flickering flames of purest hue,
A celestial show, bright and true.
In awe, we gaze at the sight,
Lost in the warmth of northern light.

Dreams are born on this cold night,
In the glow, everything feels right.
Hope ignites like fireflies,
In this vast expanse, we rise.

Each moment etched in time's embrace,
A wonder found in this place.
Together under the starlit skies,
With every heartbeat, our spirits rise.

## Celestial Paths Untraveled

Beneath the stars, paths like threads,
Whisper softly where fate treads.
Journeys call in silent night,
Through the dark, we'll find our light.

Galaxies weave tales untold,
Stories of old in stardust gold.
Every step is a new embrace,
In the vastness, find our place.

Nebulas paint in spectral dreams,
Flowing like water, moonlit beams.
We navigate through cosmic sea,
Each twinkle a call to be free.

A compass hidden in our hearts,
Guiding us to where love starts.
Untraveled paths beckon through space,
In the unknown, finding our grace.

As we wander, hopes ignite,
In every shadow, a spark so bright.
Together, we chase the night sky,
Celestial paths, just you and I.

## Enigmatic Lightscapes

In the shadows, colors bloom,
Whispers of light dispel the gloom.
Every corner, a story concealed,\nIn the dance, our fate revealed.

Shapes emerge from the unseen,
In the glow, where we have been.
Mysteries swirl in vibrant tones,
Crafting dreams from ancient stones.

Echoes linger through the night,
Enigmas shimmer, pure delight.
Flickering moments, we explore,
A tapestry we all adore.

Lightscapes shift with every breath,
Painting beauty, defying death.
In this art, our souls take flight,
Boundless journeys in radiant light.

With every glance, wonder calls,
In the labyrinth, love befalls.
Together, we weave our fate,
In enigmatic light, we resonate.

## Enchantment in the Frigid Air

Brittle whispers haunt the night,
Frosty stars, a shimmering sight.
Moonbeams dance on snow so white,
Silent magic, pure delight.

Trees adorned in icy lace,
Nature's touch, a soft embrace.
Each breath forms a clouded space,
Winter's chill, a sacred place.

Footsteps crunch beneath the hush,
Amidst the pines, a gentle rush.
Echoes linger, secrets gush,
In the stillness, hearts may hush.

Glimmering flakes like jeweled crowns,
Painting hills in frosty gowns.
Whispers weave through sleepy towns,
In this wonder, joy abounds.

Evening falls, the shadows creep,
In the beauty, silence deep.
Nature's song, a dream to keep,
In the frigid air, we leap.

## Illuminated Tranquility

A canvas brushed in pastels soft,
Whispers of light from worlds aloft.
Silent hopes through the air waft,
In stillness found, where dreams are oft.

Gentle breezes hug the trees,
Carrying scents with quiet ease.
Each moment blooms like sweet tease,
In this calm, our souls find peace.

Water glows under twilight's hand,
Reflections dance along the sand.
A symphony, life's quiet band,
In mirrored waves, dreams expand.

Stars emerge as shadows retreat,
Each twinkle holds a heart's heartbeat.
In this hush, our spirits meet,
Illuminated, life is sweet.

Sing softly, let your heart be bare,
In the glow of evening's care.
With every breath, the world we share,
In illuminated tranquility, we dare.

## Reflections of a Sky Aglow

Fiery hues at day's soft end,
Brushstrokes where the heavens blend.
Night whispers, as daylight bends,
Moments lost, yet time transcends.

Clouds ablaze in rich embrace,
A canvas filled with endless grace.
Dreams take flight in this vast space,
As daylight fades without a trace.

Rippling waves of orange and gold,
Each flicker, a story told.
In the twilight, hearts are bold,
Chasing visions, never old.

Violet shadows blend with fire,
A symphony of soft desire.
In the hush, our souls conspire,
Underneath this sky's attire.

As stars peek through the dusk's embrace,
Night unfolds, a timeless grace.
In reflections, our dreams we chase,
Beneath the sky aglow, we trace.

## **The Dance of Cosmic Colors**

Planets spin in rhythmic sway,
Electric hues in grand ballet.
Across the night, the stars display,
A cosmic dance that leads the way.

Nebulae drift like painted dreams,
In swirling patterns, soft moonbeams.
Galaxies glide on silver streams,
Infinite wonders, or so it seems.

Meteor trails streak the deep,
Promises in the darkness creep.
Whispers of secrets, they keep,
In this vastness, fears may leap.

Colors twirl with a vibrant flair,
Sketching stories in the air.
Underneath, we stand and stare,
Dancing light, a love affair.

In cosmic hues, our spirits soar,
Boundless visions to explore.
With every pulse, we seek for more,
In the dance of colors, we restore.

## Ember Dreams of the Arctic

In the quiet of the night,
Embers dance with pale light.
Whispers of the cold wind blow,
Chasing dreams of fire's glow.

Upon the snow, shadows play,
While northern lights sway and sway.
With every spark, a tale unfolds,
Of ancient hearts and winter's hold.

Fires flicker, bright and bold,
In a world of ice and cold.
They tell of warmth in icy lands,
And hope, like silver, always stands.

Underneath the star-strewn sky,
Embers breathe, they leap and fly.
Within each blaze, a secret kept,
Of dreams held tight, of tears wept.

All the frost, it dares to gleam,
Reflecting on the ember's dream.
A spark of life in frozen night,
Filling darkness with soft light.

## Flickers Above the Frost

Flickers dance on crystal frost,
Glimmers shining, never lost.
Beneath the moon's silver glance,
The night awakens, starts to dance.

Each breath of wind, a gentle sigh,
Leaves behind the stars on high.
Whispers echo through the trees,
As shadows twist, they bend with ease.

Frosty air, a biting chill,
Fires crackle, hearts will thrill.
In the dark, the warmth ignites,
Chasing dreams through endless nights.

Gold and silver, bright they gleam,
Carrying the night's sweet dream.
Above the frost, the flames will guide,
Hope and love, forever wide.

With each flicker, spirits soar,
While winter's night begins to roar.
In the dance of light and shade,
The chill of night begins to fade.

## Ethereal Lights of the Night

Ethereal lights shimmer and glow,
Painting the sky with a soft show.
Dancing wisps in the velvet air,
A magical touch, beyond compare.

Stars awaken, twinkling bright,
Guiding the dreamers through the night.
Each flicker tells a story true,
Of worlds beyond, both old and new.

In the silence, they softly beam,
Whispering secrets, a starlit dream.
With every blink, they weave their art,
Taking hold of a wandering heart.

Through shadowed paths, the lanterns lead,
Filling the void, planting a seed.
Wonders unfold with every breath,
In the realm where night dances with death.

Eternal glow, with wishes cast,
The lights above, a beauty vast.
In their gaze, we find our place,
Lost in the night's warm embrace.

## Radiance Over Frozen Waters

Radiance spills on frozen streams,
Shattering night with silver beams.
Each ripple catches a glint of light,
In the stillness, a magical sight.

Reflecting dreams on icy tides,
Nature's beauty where silence bides.
The moon dips low, kissing the frost,
In the dance with shadows, it's never lost.

Waves whisper songs of ages passed,
In the night where darkness lasts.
With every shimmer, a message clear,
Beauty lives in the heart of fear.

As dawn approaches, colors blend,
A symphony where night meets end.
The waters shimmer, a story unfolds,
Of light and peace, together it holds.

Radiant warmth hugs the cold earth,
A reminder of love, beyond worth.
In frozen waters, life can be found,
Where light and darkness gracefully surround.

## The Dance of Cosmic Fury

Stars collide in fiery grace,
Galaxies swirl in a wild chase.
Nebulas bursting, colors bright,
A cosmic waltz ignites the night.

Black holes spin, a haunting call,
Gravity's grip, we feel it all.
Time and space entwined as one,
A dance begun, never to shun.

Radiant bursts, a fiery bloom,
In endless voids, the shadows loom.
With every twirl, the universe sings,
The beauty in chaos, the joy it brings.

In the silence, the music grows,
Celestial rhythms, the cosmos knows.
Each star a note in this vast expanse,
Together they sway, in a timeless dance.

In the embrace of cosmic might,
We find our place in the infinite night.
The dance continues, forever unfurled,
A symphony born of the endless world.

## Shining Through the Whispering Pines

Moonlight weaves through branches tall,
Whispers echo, nature's call.
Pine trees sway in gentle breeze,
Nature's secrets shared with ease.

Stars above in blankets spread,
Glistening jewels, glowing thread.
The night is alive, a soft embrace,
Illuminated, find your place.

Shadows dance beneath the light,
A melody in the still of night.
Deer glide softly through the glade,
In the hush, no fears invade.

Every rustle tells a tale,
Of ancient woods and whispers pale.
In the heart of pines we roam,
Found in nature, we find home.

As dawn breaks, the pines will sigh,
Chasing dreams across the sky.
With each step, the world anew,
In the morning light, we shine through.

## **Luminous Frosted Tales**

Beneath the snow, a story lies,
Whispers of winter, gentle sighs.
Frosted branches, silent grace,
Each flake a dream, each breath a trace.

Moonlit nights in silver hue,
Painting landscapes, cold and true.
Footprints lead to places bright,
Where tales emerge in pure delight.

Crystals hang like diamond dreams,
Nature's art, in silent gleams.
Through the chill, the fire glows,
Tales of warmth, the heart bestows.

In the stillness, echoes call,
The magic wrapped in winter's thrall.
Each moment frozen, yet alive,
In frost and light, our spirits thrive.

As shadows fade, the dawn will chase,
The frosted tales, a warm embrace.
A world reborn in morning's light,
Luminous stories take their flight.

## Gentle Radiance in Midwinter

In the quiet of winter's hold,
A gentle warmth begins to unfold.
Candles flicker, shadows play,
Whispers of hope in the gray.

Snowflakes fall, a soft caress,
Blanketing earth in peaceful dress.
Each moment glows with quiet cheer,
In every heart, the light draws near.

Fires crackle, their embers glow,
Stories shared, as friendships grow.
Embraced in laughter, we gather tight,
In midwinter's chill, our spirits ignite.

The world outside may seem so still,
Yet inside, warmth we gladly fill.
With every breath, a promise made,
In gentle radiance, fears will fade.

As stars blink down, the night retreats,
With morning's light, a new heart beats.
In midwinter's hold, our love shall stay,
A gentle warmth, come what may.

## Frost and Fire Intertwined

In winter's grasp, the embers glow,
A dance of warmth in icy flow.
Snowflakes sparkle, crisp and bright,
While fire crackles, a heart's delight.

Whispers of chill caress the flame,
Each flicker speaks a lover's name.
Together they weave a tale so bold,
Of passions hot and moments cold.

The twilight's breath, a gentle sigh,
Beneath the stars, where night birds fly.
Frost kisses flames in the silent dark,
They forge a union, a radiant spark.

Within their clash, a harmony's found,
A symphony sweet with a crackling sound.
Two worlds collide, no end in sight,
In frost and fire, the soul ignites.

Endless cycles, a tender fight,
Where shadows dance in whispers light.
Eternal waltz on winter's stage,
Frost and fire, love's timeless page.

## The Night's Colorful Symphony

In velvet skies, the stars align,
Each twinkle sings, a soft design.
Moonbeams spill on the silent ground,
In this dark, magic is found.

Crickets chirp a soothing tune,
As whispers float beneath the moon.
The night unfolds its vibrant art,
A wonderland to warm the heart.

Colors swirl in the air so sweet,
Beneath the sky where dreamers meet.
Painted hues of dusk and dawn,
In every shadow, a beauty drawn.

The breeze carries secrets untold,
In this symphony, courage is bold.
Echoes of joy, like laughter ring,
As night's embrace starts to sing.

Lost in dreams, we wander free,
In the orchestra of night's decree.
Each moment glistens, each breath divine,
In the dark, the colors intertwine.

## Chasing the Celestial Mirage

On distant hills, the echoes call,
A shimmering dance, a rise and fall.
Under the skies, the dreamers tread,
With hope aflame and visions spread.

Mirage of stars, a guiding light,
Leading us through the endless night.
Chasing shadows of what could be,
In every heartbeat, a memory.

Fingers stretch towards the endless blue,
Grasping wonders that feel so true.
The cosmos whispers secrets rare,
In ethereal realms that float the air.

We wander lost, yet never far,
In the glow of a wandering star.
A tapestry woven of dreams so bright,
Chasing mirages, lost in the light.

With every step, we're drawn to fate,
In the cosmos' arms, we meditate.
The journey long, yet worth the pain,
Chasing the stars, we'll dance again.

## Shimmering Dreams in the Cold

Upon the snow, our footprints lay,
As shimmering dreams dance and sway.
Chill of the night, yet hearts grow warm,
In winter's grasp, we find our charm.

A canvas white, where stories weave,
In every flake, a hope to believe.
We chase the visions, glimmering bright,
In the frosty air, our spirits take flight.

Glistening stars above us shine,
Reflecting visions, your hand in mine.
Through icy breaths and whispered glee,
We find our magic, wild and free.

Each frozen moment, a treasure trove,
In swirling snow, our hearts will rove.
Together wrapped in a silken fold,
These shimmering dreams in the cold.

As dawn approaches with golden light,
The cold fades softly, dreams take flight.
In every heartbeat, every glance,
In the frost, we find our dance.

## Frosted Dreams Aglow

Whispers of winter dance in the night,
Frosted dreams glimmering bright.
Stars twinkle softly, a magical sight,
A world wrapped in silver, pure delight.

Snowflakes drift gently, a soft embrace,
Painting the earth with delicate grace.
In this serene, peaceful space,
Every heartbeat slows, time's gentle pace.

Moonlight cascades on the ice below,
A shimmering river, a tranquil flow.
In the quiet, hearts start to glow,
Bearing the warmth that we all know.

Beneath the canopy of night's embrace,
Frosted dreams spark a warm trace.
Hand in hand, we find our place,
In this winter's wondrous space.

Awake in the morning, the world aglow,
A canvas of white, a radiant show.
Frosted dreams linger, letting us know,
In the coldest of times, love will grow.

## Transcendent Light in the Chill

In the stillness, a promise unfolds,
Transcendent light where the heart holds.
Through frosted air, warmth gently molds,
Casting shadows in stories of old.

The chill wraps around like an old friend,
But the radiance whispers; it will not end.
Stars signal hope, on nights they depend,
Illuminating paths that twist and bend.

Through frost-kissed trees, shadows break,
Awakening dreams, a heart's gentle ache.
Beneath the silence, the soul starts to wake,
Finding solace where the frozen lake.

Glistening snow, a soft carpet lies,
Underneath the vast, enchanting skies.
Light spills freely, in nocturnal cries,
In every heartbeat, love never dies.

In moments like these, time feels so rare,
A tapestry woven with utmost care.
Transcendent light, we breathe its air,
Embracing the chill, we rise and share.

## Horizons Fired by the Cosmos

Across the sky, colors collide,
Horizons fired, with nothing to hide.
A cosmic dance, where dreams abide,
Painting the world, with stars as our guide.

In twilight moments, our spirits soar,
Every heartbeat, longing for more.
Stardust whispers from celestial lore,
Opening paths to the great beyond's door.

Glimmers of hope in the deep, dark blue,
Each shimmering star, a wish coming true.
The cosmos inspires all that we do,
In infinite patterns, both old and new.

As galaxies spin and shimmer bright,
Horizons shift in the soft twilight.
With every glance, we are filled with light,
Navigating the dark, guided by sight.

In cosmic embrace, our spirits entwine,
Horizons expanding, as dreams align.
Together we journey, hearts intertwined,
In the beauty of night, our souls divine.

## Celestial Glimmer Above the Pines

Glimmers of light through the branches peek,
Celestial whispers, soft and unique.
Underneath stars, the heart starts to speak,
Dreams take flight, no longer meek.

The night sky beckons, a velvet cloak,
Shimmering softly, as silence spoke.
Among the pines, ancient secrets evoke,
Life's gentle cycle, the universe's joke.

Love's soft warmth in the cool night air,
Celestial glimmers, a comforting prayer.
Each twinkling star becomes a flare,
Uniting souls in moments so rare.

Through forest shadows, light we chase,
Finding our path in this sacred space.
With every breath, we embrace the pace,
Written in stars, our dreams interlace.

As dawn approaches, light starts to unfurl,
Celestial dance in a cosmic whirl.
Above the pines, dreams begin to swirl,
In the heart of night, our spirits twirl.

## Spectrums of Serenity

In a meadow bright and wide,
Gentle breezes softly glide,
Colors dance and swirl around,
Whispers of peace can be found.

Beneath the sky, so vast and blue,
Nature's canvas, every hue,
Harmony in every sound,
Where joy and solace are unbound.

Blooms of blossoms, sweet and fair,
Crisp, fresh scent fills the air,
In this tranquil, sacred space,
Time stands still, embraced by grace.

As sunlight fades, a dusk unfolds,
Secrets of twilight softly told,
Stars awaken, twinkling bright,
A tapestry of pure delight.

In dreams we wander, hand in hand,
Across this softly painted land,
Together, hearts in simple glee,
In spectrums of serenity.

## Etherial Radiance

In the quiet of the night,
Moonlight weaves a silver sight,
Stars flicker with a mystic glow,
Whispers of dreams in gentle flow.

Clouds like wisps drift on high,
Dancing softly in the sky,
A symphony of cosmic light,
Guides our thoughts, sets them alight.

Crickets sing their evening song,
Nature's heart beats strong and long,
In this moment, all feels right,
Bathed in soft, ethereal light.

Winds carry secrets from afar,
Echoes of what once was star,
A connection, timeless and pure,
In this radiance, we endure.

With each breath, we find our place,
In the vastness, full of grace,
The universe cradles our dreams,
In ethereal, flowing streams.

## Midnight Murmurs in Ice

The night is deep, the world is still,
Frozen whispers, a ghostly thrill,
Moonbeams dance on icy lakes,
Chilling sighs as stillness breaks.

Crystals form in the frosty air,
Nature's breath, both bold and rare,
Each flake tells a tale untold,
Frozen secrets wrapped in cold.

Shadows flicker, come and go,
Life beneath the ice moves slow,
Midnight murmurs softly play,
In this serene disarray.

Stars reflect on surfaces bright,
A glimmering realm bathed in light,
Echoes of a world asleep,
In cold depths, mysteries creep.

Time stands still in winter's embrace,
A quiet moment, a hidden space,
In the midnight's cozy nest,
We find peace, we feel blessed.

## Glimmering Frost on Dark Waters

On dark waters, a glimmer shines,
Frosted whispers, like silver lines,
Beneath the surface, secrets sleep,
In the quiet, shadows creep.

Moonlight casts a soft caress,
Nature's wonders, we possess,
Each ripple tells a story old,
Of whispered dreams and truths untold.

Cold embraces the banks nearby,
As night weaves its velvet tie,
Stars dip low, as if to drink,
From the waters, deep we think.

In the stillness, hearts align,
Reflections trace the thoughts divine,
The frost, a tapestry so rare,
Crafted with the utmost care.

Glimmering magic fills the night,
Every shimmer feels just right,
On dark waters, united we stand,
In frosted beauty, hand in hand.

### Frost-kissed Horizons

The morning breaks, a chill in the air,
Whispers of frost cling to the trees.
Sunrise paints the world with care,
A canvas bright, a soft release.

Footprints crunch on glistening ground,
Nature's art, a fleeting show.
In quiet beauty, peace is found,
Where dreams are born, and feelings grow.

Sky stretches wide, a canvas blue,
Clouds dance lazily, drifting slow.
Every glance reveals a hue,
Of wonder wrapped in winter's glow.

As daylight fades, the stars ignite,
A silver blanket drapes the town.
Frost-kissed horizons, pure delight,
The world asleep, the sun sinks down.

In the hush, a moment stays,
Caught in time, where time stands still.
The beauty weaves through night's soft haze,
A heart at peace, a gentle thrill.

## Shards of Light in the Dark

In the stillness, shadows creep,
A world concealed, yet full of fire.
Soft beams pierce the gloom, so deep,
Igniting hope and sparking desire.

Each flicker tells a tale untold,
Of dreams that flicker, rise and fall.
With every ray, a heart unfolds,
Weaving light through darkness, enthrall.

Reflections dance on splintered glass,
Mirroring the soul's hidden quest.
Through the chaos, moments pass,
With shards of light, we find our rest.

Beneath the shroud of night's embrace,
A million stars begin to sing.
In darkest times, we find our place,
Together, we ignite and cling.

So let the shadows softly glean,
With whispers of what dreams may spark.
In the silence, truths are seen,
As we hold on to light in the dark.

## **Dreaming in the Polar Night**

Under blankets of velvety black,
Where the sun takes its long retreat,
Dreams take flight, no hint of lack,
In the stillness, our hearts compete.

Waves of auroras dance above,
A tapestry spun with care.
Embers of hope, bright like love,
Unfolding stories, rich and rare.

Frozen whispers echo through,
Nature sings a timeless tune.
In this world, made anew,
Stars beckon softly, like the moon.

Every shadow holds a sign,
Of reveries that spark the night.
In the silence, thoughts align,
Dreaming deep till morning light.

As dawn breaks, the world awakes,
Embracing all that night has shown.
In this stillness, magic wakes,
We carry dreams, forever grown.

## Echoes of Luminescent Wonder

In twilight's grasp, we hear the sound,
Of echoes weaving through the air.
A luminescent glow surrounds,
Each whisper, a song of care.

Stars beckon from their distant home,
In silver threads, we find our way.
Across the night, we choose to roam,
Where dreams and shadows softly play.

Glimmers dance on dew-kissed grass,
Illuminating paths unknown.
In every moment, memories pass,
A tapestry of light has grown.

Beneath the sky, a canvas bright,
We gather strength from nature's call.
Embraced by warmth of starlit night,
Echoes remind us we are all.

And as the dawn begins to rise,
With every hue, our spirits soar.
In echoes of luminous skies,
We find the light forevermore.

## Hues of Dusk in the Arctic

The sun dips low, a fiery glow,
Against the ice, a vibrant show.
Sky painted with colors bold,
Whispers of tales from times of old.

Shadows stretch on frozen ground,
In silence, nature's breath is found.
Each hue tells secrets of the night,
Twinkling stars ready for flight.

Crimson blush on glacial peaks,
The chill of night, the heart it speaks.
A stillness wraps the world in dreams,
As twilight weaves its softest seams.

Beneath the sky, a canvas wide,
With every shade, the world's pride.
In Arctic solace, peace unfurls,
As dusk descends on snow-kissed pearls.

A moment caught, a fleeting sigh,
Where night and day gently lie.
With each breath, we hold so dear,
The hues of dusk, forever near.

## **Whirlwind of Color Over Snow**

A dance of shades, bright and bold,
Across the white, stories told.
Whirlwinds swirl, a painter's brush,
In a vibrant, joyful rush.

Emerald greens and sapphire blues,
Mix with every bright hue.
Over fields of glistening white,
Color bursts, pure delight.

Joyful laughter fills the air,
As colors sprout, everywhere.
The world awakens, fresh and new,
In this whirlwind, life breaks through.

Twisting, turning, shades combine,
Nature's palette, truly divine.
With every gust, we feel the cheer,
As winter's grip begins to clear.

Here in the moment, we twirl and spin,
With hearts ablaze, we dance within.
A whirlwind of color, bright and free,
Over snow, we find harmony.

## Glow Beyond the Wintry Veil

A soft glow breaks through the night,
Casting dreams in silver light.
Beyond the veil of frosted air,
A warmth emerges, sweet and rare.

In depths of winter's icy hold,
A golden fire begins to unfold.
With each flicker, hope ignites,
Shattering the chill of nights.

Illuminated whispers sing,
As the heart begins to spring.
The glow invites us to believe,
In every moment, love's reprieve.

With tender hands, the night caress,
Beneath the stars, a gentle press.
In the quiet, we find our peace,
As the glow grants us sweet release.

Beyond the darkness, light will chase,
With every dawn, a warm embrace.
In winter's grip, we find our way,
To the glow that ends the fray.

## Twilight Melodies in the North

Whispers of twilight fill the air,
Melodies dance without a care.
In hush of eve, the world transforms,
As night begins its gentle norms.

From shadowed woods to starry skies,
Nature sings, her lullabies.
Each note a spark, a subtle spark,
Guiding hearts through the dark.

Beneath the moon's soft, silver gaze,
We gather round in twilight's haze.
Stories shared, with warmth they bring,
As life unfolds, and spirits sing.

Colors blend in fading light,
A symphony of day and night.
In every sigh, we hear the call,
Of twilight's charm that enchants us all.

Embracing shadows, we stand tall,
In harmony, we feel the thrall.
With every breeze, our hearts entwine,
In twilight's melodies, we find the divine.

## Whispers of the Aurora

In night's embrace, colors play,
Dancing lights in the sky's ballet.
Secrets shared in hues so bright,
Nature's song in the still of night.

Breezes sweep, stories unfold,
Whispers of magic, legends told.
Stars align in a cosmic flow,
Guiding dreams where wanderers go.

Soft glimmers of green and red,
Awakening dreams, gently spread.
Fingers reach for the ethereal,
Hopes rise high, dreams material.

Calm descends with the dawn's light,
Fading echoes of the night.
Yet in hearts, the magic stays,
Forever lingers, always plays.

Each dawn brings a new design,
A canvas bright, a grand divine.
In every heart, the aurora glows,
In whispered dreams, our spirit flows.

## **Celestial Tapestries**

Threads of light, woven so fine,
Stars create patterns, pure and divine.
Galaxies twirl in an endless dance,
A cosmic rhythm, a timeless romance.

Nebulae bloom in colors bright,
Cloaked in shadows, kissed by light.
Each constellation, a tale to share,
Charting our dreams in the midnight air.

The moon drapes silver on the sea,
Echoing whispers of destiny.
Through starlit paths, we wander free,
Guided by dreams of what might be.

In every twinkle, a wish takes flight,
Promises made in the still of night.
Tapestries woven in cosmic hues,
Connecting souls, old and new.

Celestial wonders, vast and deep,
Guarding the secrets, the universe keeps.
In the fabric of time, we find our place,
Embracing the beauty of boundless space.

# Fragments of Winter Light

Glittering crystals catch the sun,
Winter's breath, a frosty run.
Each flake unique, a fleeting grace,
In silence, they dance, a soft embrace.

Beneath the branches, shadows play,
Whispers of frost in delicate sway.
A world transformed in icy gleam,
Chasing warmth in a winter's dream.

Footsteps crunch on snow so white,
Memories swirl in soft twilight.
Candles flicker in homes so near,
Offering comfort, spreading cheer.

Stars emerge in the crisp, clear air,
Glistening diamonds, a precious pair.
Hope ignites as the night unfolds,
In fragments of light, a story told.

Nature sleeps in a quiet repose,
Wrapped in blankets where love grows.
Though winter lingers, spring takes flight,
In every heart, warmth ignites.

**Frosted Dreams at Dusk**

As the sun dips, shadows blend,
A canvas where night and day extend.
Whispers of dusk in the cool, still air,
Frosted dreams dance without a care.

Silvered leaves in twilight gleam,
Fragments of magic softly stream.
Each breath taken in the chill,
Embracing peace, a moment still.

Stars awaken in the twilight sky,
Painting memories as they sigh.
Reflections dance on the frozen lake,
In frosted dreams, life's pulse we make.

Gentle breezes carry a tune,
Singing softly to the rising moon.
In every heart, an ember glows,
Nurturing hope as the evening flows.

Dusk weaves tales of the day gone by,
In whispered tones, beneath the sky.
As night unfolds its velvet cloak,
In frosted dreams, our spirits soak.

## **Mysterious Glimmers Above**

In the still of night, they dance,
Whispers of light in a cosmic trance.
Stars flicker softly, secrets they weave,
Tales of the universe that we believe.

Shimmering orbs in the endless black,
Guiding lost souls, lighting their track.
Each twinkle a story, ancient and new,
Mysterious glimmers that draw us through.

Veiled in the dark, their beauty concealed,
In shadows of time, their truth revealed.
Nature's own canvas, painted with grace,
In the heart of the night, we find our place.

Echoes of silence, they softly ignite,
Dreams in the heavens, a sublime sight.
Catch a glimpse of the grand design,
In the celestial ballet, we intertwine.

From dusk until dawn, they twinkle and shine,
A connection to worlds, both yours and mine.
So look to the sky, let your spirit roam,
In mysterious glimmers, you'll find your home.

## A Ballet of Fire in the Sky

Adrift on the wind, colors collide,
A ballet of fire, a celestial tide.
Red, orange, and gold, a glorious show,
Painted by dusk, where the wild winds blow.

As the sun dips low, the horizon ignites,
With hues that flicker like dazzling lights.
Every moment a marvel, a fleeting delight,
Nature's own stage, where day meets night.

Clouds waltz through the air, so soft and profound,
Casting shadows and shapes all around.
In the twilight hour, enchantments arise,
A dance of the heavens, a feast for the eyes.

Each flicker, a heartbeat, a transient spark,
Illuminating dreams when the skies go dark.
Awakening spirits in the dying day,
As fireflies gather, then gently sway.

So let us be still, catch the magic that flies,
In a ballet of fire, beneath painted skies.
Let's whisper our wishes as daylight takes flight,
In the arms of the evening, our hearts feel light.

## **Lightplay Over Snowy Fields**

A frosty blanket, pure and bright,
Where shadows dance in the silver light.
Gentle whispers of the winter's breeze,
Playful glimmers among the trees.

Sunbeams twinkle on icy crowns,
Transforming the world, spinning round town.
Crystal shards glitter, a magical sight,
With every step, the snow feels light.

Children's laughter echoes afar,
With snowflakes swirling like tiny stars.
Each moment caught in a fleeting glow,
Painting their dreams where the cold winds blow.

Footprints left in the powdery snow,
A treasure of memories, gentle and slow.
In the quietude of winter's embrace,
Lightplay enchants this serene space.

As twilight descends, the night unveils,
A canvas of wonder, the moonlight sails.
In the stillness, we breathe, lost in the chill,
In lightplay over fields, our hearts are filled.

## **Luminous Secrets of the Arctic**

In frosty depths where silence reigns,
Luminous secrets, nature's chains.
Auroras dance in green and blue,
Whispering tales to the bold and true.

Icebergs drift in twilight's glow,
Guardians of mysteries lying below.
With every shimmer, the myths reside,
In the heart of the Arctic, where dreams abide.

Whales sing softly, beneath the tide,
Echoes of wisdom in currents wide.
Frozen landscapes cradle their song,
Resonating futures that stretch so long.

The stars appear, a canvas so vast,
Reminders of ages and shadows cast.
In the hush of the night, ancient stories rise,
In luminous secrets, we seek the wise.

So let us wander where the ice meets the sea,
Discovering wonders born wild and free.
Amidst the bright hues that the sky does paint,
Luminous secrets we cherish, we saint.

## The Chill of Radiance

A whisper in the winter air,
Where moonlight dances, soft and fair.
The stars, they twinkle, bright and cold,
As secrets of the night unfold.

Frosty breaths in silence creep,
Beneath the shadows, secrets seep.
The world adorned in silver lace,
Each corner holds a hidden grace.

The chill embraces every dream,
In every glance, the starlight beams.
A quiet thrill, a tranquil peace,
Where hearts in solitude find release.

The echoes of the night resound,
In every sigh, a magic found.
Embraced by dusk, we wander blind,
In radiance, the truth we find.

So let us revel in the night,
Each moment drenched in pure delight.
For in the chill, the warmth we trace,
A symphony of starry grace.

## Shards of Crystal Blue

In fractured light, reflections play,
Each shard a story, bright and gay.
A world in pieces, yet so whole,
Glimmers that awaken the soul.

Through azure depths, the whispers hum,
A melody from waters' drum.
Beneath the surface, dreams collide,
Where every heartbeat flows with pride.

The crystal shards like fireflies,
Illuminate the night skies.
With every flicker, colors bloom,
A dance of light dispelling gloom.

In every choice, in every glance,
We find the spark, we find the chance.
To gather shards and forge anew,
The vision bright, the crystal blue.

So let us hold these pieces tight,
Transforming darkness into light.
For in the fragments, hope is found,
In crystal blue, our dreams abound.

## Silence Beneath the Cosmic Glow

In silence deep, the cosmos hums,
With every pulse, the universe drums.
The stars align in quiet grace,
In vast expanses, we find our place.

Beneath the glow, the shadows sway,
In starlit whispers, night holds sway.
The gentle breeze, a lullaby,
That carries wishes through the sky.

Each comet's trail, a fleeting chance,
To dream anew, to take a stance.
The night, a canvas, dark and wide,
Across its depths, our hopes collide.

In cosmic silence, truths arise,
And from the void, our spirits fly.
With every star, a story told,
In radiant light, our hearts unfold.

So let us linger, lost and found,
In silence deep, a sacred sound.
For beneath the glow, our souls will grow,
In harmony with the cosmic flow.

## Elysian Lights Over January

Amidst the frost, the heavens gleam,
With Elysian lights, we weave a dream.
January whispers, soft and bright,
As dawn awakens the winning light.

A tapestry of gold and blue,
Each thread a moment, pure and true.
In winter's grasp, we find a song,
With every heartbeat, we belong.

The days unfold like petals wide,
In subtle grace, the stars abide.
With every breath, the year's reborn,
In Elysian glow, we greet the dawn.

So let the chill wrap round us tight,
As warmth ignites the frigid night.
In January's glow, we dare to see,
The beauty in what's yet to be.

For in the lights that dance above,
We find the echoes of our love.
Through every season, bright or gray,
Elysian lights will guide our way.

## Vivid Ruins of Frost

In the silence of the night,
Whispers of ice take flight.
Branches tangled, silver bright,
Lost in dreams, a ghostly sight.

Crystals crown the barren trees,
Echoes dance on frosty breeze.
Colors fade like ancient pleas,
Time stands still, the world at ease.

Beneath the moon's soft embrace,
Nature wears a frozen lace.
Footsteps fade without a trace,
In the chill, we find our place.

Moonlight glistens on the ground,
In this stillness, peace is found.
In the ruins, beauty'sound,
Nature's art, profound, unbound.

Every flake, a story told,
Whispers of a winter bold.
In the dawn, the frost will hold,
Memories of a world of cold.

## **Pale Flames on a Winter's Breath**

Softly flickers, shadows dance,
In the heart's warm, fleeting chance.
Pale flames reflect a winter's glance,
Moments lost in sweet romance.

Frosty air, it bites so keen,
Yet the fire's glow is seen.
Winter's chill, a silver sheen,
In the depths, warmth's evergreen.

Dancing embers, stories spark,
Lighting up the endless dark.
Each soft whisper leaves a mark,
In the night, where dreams embark.

Through the veil of icy dreams,
Hope survives in flickered beams.
Hearts unite in gentle themes,
Pale flames glowing, love redeems.

Winter winds may freeze the air,
But love's fire provides a flare.
In the hush, a tender prayer,
Holding close, beyond compare.

## Frigid Firefly Reverie

In a world of frozen light,
Fireflies twinkle, small and bright.
Whispers hitch a chilly flight,
Dreams unfold in velvet night.

Beneath the stars, the silence glows,
As the frosty wind softly blows.
In this reverie, time slows,
Magic in the stillness flows.

Snowflakes fall like whispered dreams,
Glistening in the silver beams.
Nature's breath, a hush that seems,
Cloaked in dreams, a world that teems.

Frigid sparks dance in the air,
In this night, we shed our care.
With each flicker, hearts laid bare,
Lost in dreams, a love affair.

In the calm, the echoes blend,
Each bright light, a wish to send.
Frozen moments never end,
In this peace, our hearts commend.

## **Ribbons in the Crystal Air**

Softly weaving through the frost,
Ribbons fly, no moment lost.
Nature's art, at what cost?
In the chill, our warmth embossed.

Patterns twirl in winter's hand,
Windswept dreams across the land.
In the stillness, we shall stand,
Bound by threads, a fate unplanned.

Glimmers on the icy ground,
In this dance, new hopes are found.
Through the chill, our hearts resound,
In the beauty, joy unbound.

Every twist a tale to tell,
In the echoes, ours to dwell.
In the frosty, luminous spell,
Ribbons swirl, as dreams compel.

In the night's embrace, we soar,
Through the patterns, evermore.
Crystal visions to explore,
In this dance, our spirits roar.

## Colors of the Cold Night

The moon glows silver in the air,
Whispers of frost, a delicate flare.
Shadows dance on the icy ground,
In this quiet beauty, peace is found.

Stars twinkle like gems in the dark,
Each a story, a hidden spark.
The chill wraps round with a gentle sigh,
Under this tapestry, we wonder why.

The night wears hues of deep, dark blue,
With hints of purple, a mystic hue.
Breath visible in the crisp, cool air,
We stand in awe, in silent prayer.

Drifts of snow fall soft and light,
Painting the world, a dreamlike sight.
Every flake unique, a delicate lace,
In the colors of the cold night's embrace.

Under the stars, we find our way,
Guided by hope, through night and day.
In the colors that only winter brings,
We gather joy, the heart sings.

## The Celestial Canvas

Upon the sky, a vast expanse,
The stars converge, a cosmic dance.
Brushstrokes of light on a deep, dark sea,
Painting our dreams, wild and free.

Nebulas swirl in colors bright,
Merging shadows with purest light.
Galaxies spin in a grand array,
As time whispers softly, night turns to day.

Comets blaze with a brilliant tail,
Stories of old in every trail.
Shooting stars, wishes on the wing,
In this vast canvas, hope takes wing.

Constellations tell tales of old,
Maps of the skies, secrets untold.
Ancient myths in the starlight gleam,
In the celestial canvas, we dare to dream.

The universe sings in a cosmic tune,
Each body of light, a radiant boon.
We gaze in wonder, hearts intertwined,
Lost in the beauty, our spirits aligned.

## When Stars Take Flight

In the evening's gentle hush,
Stars awaken, a silent rush.
They rise like dreams into the night,
Dancing together, pure delight.

With each twinkle, a story told,
Wishes released, a magic bold.
Shooting stars streak across the sky,
Silent reminders that dreams can fly.

The universe opens its boundless door,
As constellations beckon us to explore.
In the quiet, we find our place,
In the realm where the stars embrace.

Moonlight bathes the world in grace,
As shadows play in a timeless space.
Hearts lifted high, we cannot fight,
The pull of wonder when stars take flight.

Together we stand, hands in hands,
Bound by the night, our future expands.
Under this sky, where dreams ignite,
We find our hope when stars take flight.

## **Heartbeat of the Frozen Sky**

Whispers of winter in the air,
A heartbeat soft, a timeless prayer.
The sky, a canvas of pale, pale blue,
In its embrace, our hearts renew.

Crystals glitter in the morning light,
A frozen chorus, pure and bright.
The world is still, as if in thought,
In this frozen realm, all battles fought.

Every breath a cloud, every step a song,
In the silence, we all belong.
Time dances gently, slow and wide,
In the heartbeat of the frozen sky, we bide.

Chasing warmth beneath the sun's gaze,
In the chill, we find our ways.
Embracing snow's soft, white delight,
In the heartbeat of the frozen night.

Together we stand, "forever," we vow,
In the shimmering beauty of the here and now.
With hearts so full, we dare to fly,
In the moment's pulse, beneath the sky.

Milton Keynes UK
Ingram Content Group UK Ltd.
UKHW010229111224
452348UK00011B/602